# WILD ABOUT
# The Wetlands

## A YEAR IN THE LIFE OF THE LONDON WETLAND CENTRE

### By Andrew Wilson

Historian: Caroline MacMillan

**WWT**

Kindly supported by:

*To my lovely wife, Diana, my number one supporter.*

# Foreword

Tucked away in a loop of the River Thames, in the heart of the great city of London, is the WWT London Wetland Centre. It may be surrounded by houses and busy roads, but it is an oasis of tranquillity for people and wildlife alike – and, without doubt, it's my favourite place in the capital.

A magical world of lakes, reedbeds and gardens, it brings the countryside to London. Within its 40 hectares, I've seen everything from kingfishers and black-tailed godwits to slow worms and at least a dozen species of butterflies. I had my best ever sighting of a water vole in a delightfully quiet corner of the reserve, and once spent a very happy morning listening to the evocative sound of a booming bittern. I have jealously viewed it from the air on many occasions, too, wishing I was wildlife watching in the haven below instead of coming in to land in what felt like the parallel universe of Heathrow.

This isn't urban wildlife in the traditional sense. It is nature at its very best – with some of the finest wildlife the country has to offer. While the world's precious wetlands are vanishing at an alarming rate, here WWT has turned the tide to ensure that wildlife in this unique sanctuary will flourish for generations to come.

Even if you're not a wildlife enthusiast (at least, not yet – I'm sure you will be after a few visits) it's the perfect place for a relaxing walk along the meandering paths. Or it's somewhere to sit and contemplate, immersing yourself in the sights, sounds and scents of nature, away from the hustle and bustle of the city.

The centre celebrates its 21st anniversary this year, so it's splendid to have a book that honours such a phenomenal success. Andrew has captured the essence of this wonderful slice of urban wilderness with his fabulous collection of photographs. He knows the reserve well – and it shows. He has clearly spent an inordinate amount of time capturing some truly wonderful images and the result is a sensational celebration of the jewel in London's crown.

I've been a huge fan of WWT and its innovative, well-informed and critical work ever since its founder, Peter Scott, kindly took me under his wing when I was just starting out in conservation at the age of 21. He introduced me to his beloved Wildfowl & Wetlands Trust and I have followed and supported its work closely ever since. I know he would have been immensely proud of the WWT London Wetland Centre and everything it has achieved.

So do enjoy the book – and please support WWT and its life-changing work in any way you can.

**Mark Carwardine**
Vice President

**The Four Seasons - Clockwise from Top Left:**
Winter, spring, summer and autumn

# Contents

# Welcome to The Wetlands

Welcome to my latest book in my village series, which is my most ambitious that I have published to date. I have been a member of The Wetland Centre in Barnes ever since it opened back in 2000, so you could say that this is very much a passion project. Not without its challenges, Covid being just one, it has been a wonderful experience and an absolute thrill to be able to share my love of nature with you.

Three years in the making, it's never a one man show and there are many people to thank for their help along the way. My historian, Caroline MacMillan, who I have been working with for the last 7 years and for which this will be our 7th book. I have dealt with a whole host of WWT staff, unfortunately, far too many to name them all here but I would like to single out Lisa Woodward, the general manager, Sebastien Latour, retail manager, Corinne Pluchino, director of marketing and Barnaby Briggs, the chairman of the trustees. Also, a special thank you to Nick and Huw, who on numerous occasions let me in at some ungodly hour to take some pictures.

I would also like to thank Mark Carwardine, vice president of WWT, for kindly providing such an evocative foreword for the book, and Gyles Brandreth and Frank Gardner for their seasonal quotes. Finally, I would like to thank my sponsors for kindly helping me. For good reason, my books are of the highest quality, which comes at a price and I can't thank Berkeley Homes, Denmaur Paper and Chestertons more for their most generous help.

There are also numerous other people I have met along the way, some of whom are mentioned in the book, who have either directly helped me, or given me inspiration from time to time and I would love to thank you all, you know who you are. Lastly, a quick plug for my designer, Kieran Metcalfe, a fine photographer himself (and one of the reasons I asked him to help me in the first place), who kindly puts up with my sometimes strange way of doing things.

Many people say to me that the sun is always shining in my books and I hope that you experience some of this warmth too.

**Andrew Wilson**
September 2021

Since I started my series of books back in 2009, our family springer spaniel, Josie, has been a feature of all my books. Sadly, she is now over 15 and nowhere near as sprightly as she used to be. So it is just as well that WWT don't allow dogs in. I was sure I had a picture of her sat by the gates whilst I nipped in for a picture. However, I couldn't find that but I thought this picture from a few years ago of her racing through water was more appropriate.

# London Wetland Centre

As the Thames slowly loops through the busy metropolis and tidal water glides quietly under Hammersmith's magnificent Victorian bridge, passengers in planes heading towards their final destination at Heathrow Airport may look down and catch sight of a green space below. They might see a patchwork of pools and small lagoons with the evening sun glinting on the silvery surface. Some will wonder why this open area bordering the southern bank of the river and surrounded by a mass of urban roads and houses has never been covered by bricks and mortar, others may recognise it as Barn Elms, one of nature's jewels in the heart of a major city and home to the

Wetland Centre. But how did this area of natural beauty arrive in London?

The West Middlesex Water Works purchased Barn Elms Farm in the 1890s and built four reservoirs to supply water to London, but nearly a hundred years later the large tanks were redundant and the area had become a Site of Special Scientific Interest with a large number of wildfowl wintering there. Under the Water Industries Act the owners, Thames Water, were obliged to conserve and enhance the natural interest of the site and started negotiations with the Wildfowl and Wetlands Trust which had been founded by Sir Peter Scott. He had already established a wildfowl sanctuary at

Slimbridge overlooking the Severn estuary and dreamed of creating one in London which would introduce city dwellers to the wonders of nature and conservation. It is interesting to note that while researching this book I discovered that local resident, Gyles Brandreth, played a leading role here. His friend, none other than Prince Philip, suggested that in order to preserve the reservoirs he might like to talk to his friend, Sir Peter Scott – the rest, as they say, is history.

By 1989 negotiations were under way with Thames Water and the Wetlands Trust and when Berkeley Homes, a respected residential building company bought a corner of the site to build luxury houses and also donate eleven million pounds, the planning and design for the site started.

A team of engineers, scientists, architects and ecologists worked with the Wetlands Trust and when the centre was opened by Sir David Attenborough in May 2000 it had been transformed into a series of open water lakes, ponds, pools and reedbeds. A grazing marsh was designed to flood in winter months attracting ducks and other wildfowl whilst islands covered in vegetation became nesting sanctuaries during breeding time. A wide range of aquatic and herbaceous plants were carefully researched in order to attract the wildlife and thousands of trees and

**Left:** The four reservoirs before construction started

The entrance to Queen Elizabeth walk earlier last century when it was
The Ranelagh Club (above left) and as it is today (above right)

shrubs were carefully planted. A pond zone was housed in a thatched round house, boardwalks wound through woodland and hides became peaceful birdwatching havens.

A visitor centre welcomed visitors and its glass observatory gave sweeping views across the entire reserve.

Gradually wildlife arrived, migrating birds came for the winter months while new visitors such as lapwings settled in and have been breeding here ever since.  It became a feeding ground for a variety of bats and dragonflies and an unexpected plant, Marsh Dock, arrived under its own steam.  Arriving at the centre is a wonderful bronze statue of Sir Peter Scott standing at the water's edge, in his hand he is drawing the wildfowl he so loved with two Bewick's swans at his feet. Peter Scott's dream had become reality and as the amount of wildlife visitors has increased so too have the human ones who come to learn about wetland habitats and enjoy this haven of conservation in the heart of a busy city.

# The Wetland Centre
A vision of London's premier wetland

## The Past

The Wetland Centre is being created from four former reservoirs which were no longer required thanks to the introduction of the Thames Water Ring Main. The reservoirs had become very important for migratory and resident birds and were designated a Site of Special Scientific Interest (SSSI) in 1975. As it was not practical to maintain these reservoirs, it was decided by Thames Water to find a sympathetic use for the land and today's scheme was developed in conjunction with WWT. The creation of The Wetland Centre is funded through the sale of new homes built by Berkeley Homes on part of the site.

Thames Waterside

Construction site

## The Present

Originally conceived by Sir Peter Scott, founder of The Wildfowl & Wetlands Trust, The Wetland Centre has been a co-operative project by WWT ecologists, landscape architects Scott-Wilson Resource Consultants, consulting engineers Lewin Fryer and Partners, civil engineers Cinnamond Reclamation Ltd. and Thames Water.
The buildings have been designed by architects John Thompson and Partners. Wildlife monitoring is being supported by English Nature, WWF and the Environment Agency.

Gradually all the reservoirs have been broken up, to be replaced by a complex of lakes, ponds, reedbeds and shallow flooded wetlands. This phase of the work has been completed, with planting continuing for the next two years. Construction work on the Peter Scott Centre commences in 1997 and it is expected that The Wetland Centre will open to the public in the year 2000.

This innovative urban development will create an oasis for wetland wildlife just four miles from Hyde Park Corner.

## The Future

Artists impression

Visitors will be able to see scores of wild birds in beautiful and accessible surroundings as well as being able to find out more about the environment. The latest technology will be used, including a fibre optic cabling system part sponsored by Telewest Communications (London South) Ltd.
This will relay pictures of nesting and feeding birds on the reserve to screens in the Peter Scott Centre.

WWT is also seeking additional funding to add to the educational value of The Wetland Centre.
Plans include:
Thames Riverlife – the story of the wildlife of the Thames from source to sea,
An Ecodome – a temperature-controlled building interpreting tropical wetlands, and
A conservation centre – with facilities for environmental training and community use.

**Above:** This leaflet was kindly lent to me by Fred London, who I met over the course of preparing this book. Fred used to work for JTP the architects, who were master planners for the residential scheme, Barnes Waterside, and architects for the visitor centre. Fred is retired now but it was fascinating discovering how they took Sir Peter's vision for the reserve and help bring it to life.

# Barn Elms Estate
## A brief history of the site

The Barn Elms estate dates back to the 11th century when the Archbishop of Canterbury granted land south of the river to the Dean and Chapter of St Paul's cathedral. The area remained relatively rural until 1579 when Queen Elizabeth I bought the lease from the clergy and gave it to her principal secretary, Sir Francis Walsingham. Born into a well-connected family, at the age of twenty Walsingham had studied at Cambridge University and after travelling in Europe embarked on a career in law and is best remembered as her 'spymaster', running a network of spies throughout England and Europe. Walsingham built a mansion here and the Queen visited him several times.

By 1694 Thomas Cartwright had demolished the medieval manor and erected an impressive mansion facing the river surrounded by expansive parkland which was more in keeping with the times. George Frederick Handel stayed at the mansion in 1713 and when Count Heidegger, master of the King's revels entertained George II it was described as 'an evening of delight'. The estate was purchased by Sir Richard Hoare of the banking family, two wings were added to the house and the family lived there for over fifty years.

The house was finally taken by the prestigious Ranelagh Polo Club from Fulham, the manor became a popular sporting venue and clubhouse. The estate contained four polo grounds, ten croquet lawns, two tennis courts, an eighteen-hole golf course and two lakes for rowing. Eventually membership of the club declined and during war time the polo pitches turned into allotments under the Dig for Victory Scheme. In 1954 the now dilapidated club house burned down so the lake was drained, an athletic track built and the remainder of the grounds converted into playing fields.

There had previously been two other houses close to the mansion, one called Queen Elizabeth's Dairy belonged to Jacob Tonson, a bookseller and founder of the Kit-Kat Club and a room was specially built for their meetings. The purpose of the club was to discuss literature but often the subject was more political than art. Many of the members had their portrait painted by another member, Sir Godfrey Kneller, who presented them to Tonson and several of them now hang in the National Portrait Gallery.

Just to the north of Barn Elms mansion lay Home Farm. William Cobbett came from a farming family, served in the army and became a political activist and in 1827 leased the farm to carry out experiments in growing maize instead of potatoes and a form of self-supporting husbandry. His workmen were paid in kind rather than money and he so upset his domestic servants that few stayed long. After three years, much to the relief of his staff, he gave up farming and became the Member of Parliament for Oldham. Home Farm's last owner was Francis Trowell, the family continued farming the land until 1894 when the West Middlesex Water Works purchased the land and built four reservoirs. Just over a hundred years later the entire area of the Barn Elms estate had been developed for housing or recreational use and the now redundant reservoirs opened as the London Wetland Centre.

## Barn Elms Playing Fields

Once the largest polo club in the world, The Ranelagh Club moved from Fulham to the former Barn Elms estate in the 1880s and remained there until just before the Second World War. When the dilapidated club house burned down in 1954 the surrounding parkland was converted into school playing fields but the threat that the wide-open green spaces could be sold off for development alarmed local residents. Gyles Brandreth lived close by and was chairman of the National Playing Fields Association and together with local residents founded the Barn Elms Protection Association. Several other campaigning groups were formed including the Barn Elms Sports Trust and, with the approval of Richmond Council, in 2013 they were awarded a contract to protect the fields for public use for the next 199 years.

An athletic track was built, cricket, rugby and football pitches laid out, a state-of-the-art pavilion erected and a former lake, Shadwell's Pool, became home to the Barnes and Mortlake Angling and Preservation Society.

## Barnes Waterside

It was the foresight of the late Tony Pidgley, a well-respected home builder, who saw the potential for developing part of the open land overlooking the Thames by Hammersmith Bridge. Berkeley Homes bought a corner where the filter beds and pumping station originally stood and generously donated eleven million pounds to the neighbouring Wetland Centre. The area was carefully laid out with several apartment buildings overlooking the river, tree lined roads of terraced houses were tastefully built and a landscaped lake surrounded by elegant town houses.

**Caroline MacMillan**
June 2021

Barn Elms Athletics Track

Barnes Waterside from the Wildside Hide

# The Reserve from the Air

The Wildside

Living Collection

Main Lake

Visitor Centre
& Main Entrance

Peacock Tower

Sheltered Lagoon

South Side

# Winter

Wintertime is used to maintain and control the trees on the reserve, as the absence of foliage makes the coppicing much easier. Areas are divided into blocks and some trees are felled at the base to prevent the scrub developing into mature woodland. The resultant open areas enable light to reach the cleared ground and the remaining individual trees to develop healthily. It also increases biodiversity as the increased light reaching the ground allows other species to grow there which in turn are food sources for butterflies and other insects.

I love winter for one simple reason: the light. Despite the colder temperatures, winter light can have a wonderful clarity and a gorgeous warm hue, the sky is often more dramatic and shadows are more shadowy (unlike the less than theatrical shadows of summer). Even the birds tend to be sporting their brightest plumage. It's photography heaven.

**MARK CARWARDINE**
Vice President

It hasn't snowed at the Centre for some years now. When it did in early 2021 there was restricted access, so these pictures are taken from my archives and prove how beautiful the place can be when it does.

# Christmas at The Wetlands

Christmas is a special time for everyone and Barnes is no different. The centre puts on extra activities for families, from Father Christmas to the huge boot that greets everyone on arrival. In 2019 they put on some husky rides, which proved very popular (see page 22).

# Beautiful Winter Light

The flock of cormorants flying across the lake in late winter afternoon sunshine can be quite spectacular. **Overleaf:** The sheltered lagoon at dusk.

One of the most iconic winter visitors to the wetlands is the wonderful bittern. Part of the heron family, they are shy birds and ideally suited to life in the reeds, blending in extremely well. As a consequence, they can be incredibly difficult to spot - see if you can make him or her out in the top picture. Reliant on marshland and in particular reed beds, they are a threatened species and we are lucky to have them.

**Opposite Bottom:** A pair of pochards, with the colourful male on the left.

**Previous Page and Opposite:** The great crested grebe. **Above:** The sun going down over the sheltered lagoon.

**This page:** The black-headed gull is amongst the smaller of our British gulls and a great success at the reserve, as with many places elsewhere in the UK. Breeding in great numbers they have sadly displaced the rather prettier terns that also try and breed here. In summer they have chocolate hoods that cover their faces which disappear in winter, just leaving a small black patch behind the eye, see above.

**Overleaf:** A cormorant, showing the brightly-coloured skin around the face which they develop in the breeding season.

Whatever the time of year, the resident family of birds, found within the Living Collection, is a popular feature for the children, especially at feeding time.

**This Page, Top:** Lesser whistling duck from Asia.

**Bottom:** The rather beautiful Puna teal from South America.

# The Fabulous Lapwing

Resident all year round and also with a few breeding pairs, the fabulous lapwing can be found in much larger flocks in winter, taking advantage of the milder weather. Appearing black and white, it is only when you get up closer do you spot the lovely iridescent colouring around its neck and body. Also called the peewit, on account of its distinctive call, they are quite a sight when flying in large groups.

# The Reserve in the Fog

Watching the action...

# Accessibility

The reserve is an excellent place for anyone in a wheelchair as the ground is perfectly flat and the paths are very smooth. I am grateful to a good friend of mine, Sarah, for being my model for the day and there's nothing she likes better than a good day out with her camera observing a bit of bird life. We were lucky with the weather in March and saw plenty of action including shovelers (top right) and some wigeon (bottom right).

There are several pairs of mute swans on the reserve and they are known to be very territorial, so each separate lake has its own pair.

Off home after
a wonderful day

# Spring

During spring time information is carefully collected to monitor the breeding of waders and ducks. The nests are regularly surveyed, and the number of young chicks counted. The resultant data helps establish the breeding pattern of the various species and whether their overall productivity is increasing year by year.

Snake's-head fritillary, with their elegant bell-shaped flowers, are seen at their best from April until the middle of May. The reserve is also awash with the little yellow cowslips at this time.

Nothing is so beautiful as Spring –
When weeds, in wheels, shoot long and lovely and lush;
Thrush's eggs look little low heavens, and thrush
Through the echoing timber does so rinse and wring
The ear, it strikes like lightnings to hear him sing;
The glassy peartree leaves and blooms, they brush
The descending blue; that blue is all in a rush
With richness; the racing lambs too have fair their fling.

Gerard Manley Hopkins (1844–1899) was right: nothing is so beautiful as Spring – the season of rebirth and renewal and my favourite time to wander through the extraordinary Wildfowl and Wetlands Trust in Barnes, listening to the enchanting song of the chiffchaff, catching sight of the mammals that have mated in the winter and are now giving birth, meeting the tiny ducklings and fledgling birds, and (for me, almost best of all) simply breathing in the light fragrance of the wild flowers. Spring is sprung, God's in her heaven, and in London SW13 at least, all's well with the world.

GYLES BRANDRETH
(Past chairman of the Barn Elms Protection Association who met with Sir Peter Scott at Slimbridge in the late 80s to discuss the idea of founding The Wetland Centre in Barnes.)

# Back at Last

After three lockdowns due to Covid, April 12 2021 could not come quick enough for the fans of the reserve at Barnes and what a beautiful day it was. Even the swans were curious to meet us, almost as if they had missed our company.

As the days lengthen, visitors are met with the joyful sight of cowslips appearing all over the reserve

# Blackthorn & Blossom

The coming of spring is heralded by the most glorious show of blossom, which everyone and everything seems to enjoy.

**Clockwise from Top Left:** Orange tip butterfly, beefly, blue tit and chiffchaff.

**Clockwise from Top Left:** Small tortoiseshell butterfly, peacock butterfly, blue tit and blackcap.

As spring arrives, the birds on the reserve pair up and nest. This seems to include a lot of fighting, especially amongst the resident coots, and the swans have a particular dislike for the Canada geese (see previous page).

**This Page, Clockwise from Top Left:** Coots, Canada goose and a very angry male mandarin duck. **Opposite Page, Clockwise from Top Left:** Male mallard ducks, coots, a pair of shoveler ducks, a male shoveler duck.

# Great Crested Grebes

One of the most wonderful spectacles to be found in the bird world has to be the extraordinary courtship display of the great crested grebe. Besides being the most beautiful of birds, to witness them bobbing their heads about, extending their crests and then passing weeds to one another is a magical sight.

The great crested grebe is an excellent fisherman. I was also pleased to discover one of their nests hidden away in the reeds, bottom left, and if I hadn't been watching them for sometime, I would never have spotted it as it is really well camouflaged. Sadly, this nest wasn't a success.

79

The blacked-headed gulls, opposite page, are very greedy with the best nesting spots, leaving the poor terns with little or no space. The moorhens, this page, can be funny and apart from collaborating as family units, so adolescents from previous broods helping out, they also choose some of the most bizarre nesting sites. Although very precarious, it proved to be the perfect nesting place to raise their family.

This mallard was less fortunate in her choice of nest venue, next to the path by the main buildings (below top left and right). Needless to say it failed. The pair of swans that inhabit the ponds as you arrive looked at many places to build their nest, even under Sir Peter Scott's statue, but in the end chose a spot out of site amongst the reeds.

The coots are another success story on the reserve with every pool and pond containing a nest. They are very feisty and territorial and don't allow other coots to share their patch.

# Spring Flowers

The reserve in Barnes is not just about the animals, it is also a haven for plants.

**This Page, Clockwise from Top Left:** Marsh marigolds, cuckoo flower (sometimes known as lady's smock), reeds and willow blossom.

**Opposite Page:** Perennial favourite, the fritillaries are part of the lily family.

There was some terrific news in the spring of 2021 when it was announced that the sand-martin bank, which can be found at the east end of the reserve, with the best views from the wader-scrape hide, had almost full occupancy for the first time in its history.

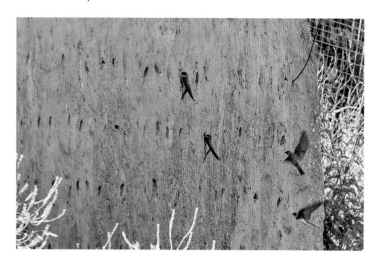

# The Kids' Zone

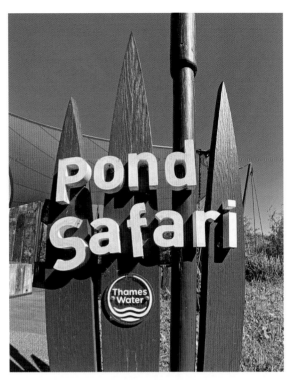

As a family friendly destination, there is lots for children to do on the reserve. Some of it organised, like the regular sessions of pond dipping and other places like the adventure area on the south side up by the sheltered lagoon. As they go around, there are also other things to see such as the wonderful Lego animals. Being a wild reserve, you never know who might drop in on the fun.

**Clockwise from Top Left:** A pied wagtail (look carefully and you can see the insects he has his eye on), a young moorhen and a ring-necked parakeet

# Amphibians

Always a favourite, there are many frogs on the reserve, although you are more likely to hear the plop of water as they escape your view rather than actually see them. Amphibians, unlike reptiles, require water to breed and you'll find common frogs (this page and overleaf), marsh frogs (the noisy ones) and newts on site.

**Below:** I put out an appeal earlier this year for any pictures that visitors to the reserve had taken, from the amusing to the rare. I am grateful to Maureen Rhodes for having sent me this rather fun one.

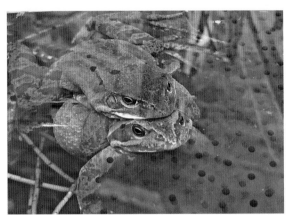
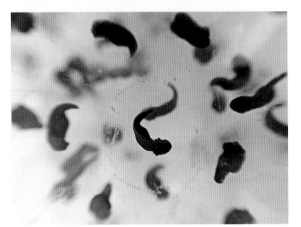

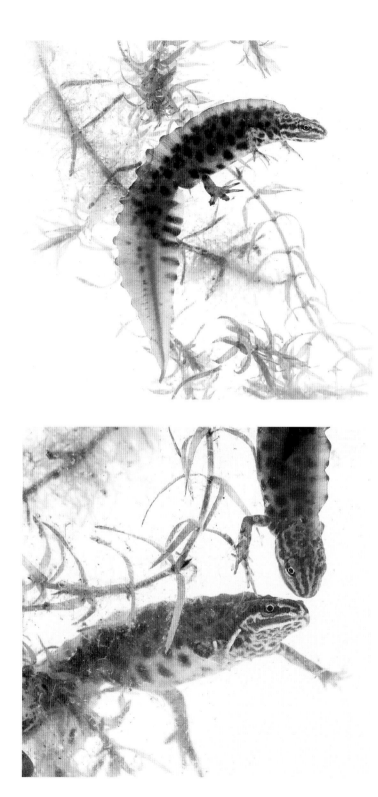

**Opposite Page, Top Left, Right and Bottom Left:** Marsh frogs. **Middle Right:** common frogs amongst some newly lain frogspawn. **Bottom Right:** A tadpole forming.

**This Page:** Great crested newts.

With the multitude of nests across the reserve, the visitor is finally rewarded with the wonderful sight of babies everywhere. Ducklings, as seen on this page, seem to be born with the knowledge that they need to chase flies.

**Opposite Page:** Coots are very successful breeders on the reserve but as parents, they can display unusual behaviour, here seen picking up their young by the head and swinging them around (bottom left and middle).

**This Page, Top:** Moorhens are another success story, with some appearing almost around every corner.

**Bottom Left:** Female tufted duck with young.

**Bottom Right:** Canada geese family outside the main building.

Without doubt, one of the more popular attractions at the reserve is the pair of Asian short-clawed otters, the smallest of the otter family. Unlike their UK relatives, they are active during the day and can be seen playing, eating and even sleeping out in the open.

Another feature of the otter area, is the grey heron that can be seen in the pen most days, looking out for an easy meal.

# Damselflies

We have as many as 20 different damselflies in the UK, with the most common, certainly at the reserve, being the common blue (see this page). The large red can be seen overleaf. Thinner than their cousins the dragonflies, their presence can be an indication of the quality of the water. Starting life as a nymph in water they are predators, preying on other insects.

# Buttercups & Daisies

Such simple flowers but so beautiful and the meadows become a mass of gold and white.

**Clockwise from Top Left:** Green-veined white butterfly, red-breasted goose, young moorhen, mother-shipton day flying moth, mallard duck with her one duckling, moorhen, barnacle goose and male mallard duck.

**Overleaf:** The Dulverton Hide.

# The Living Collection

For years WWT have done valuable work behind the scenes to protect bird species from across the world, as well as back here in the UK. Some of this work is reflected in the exhibits in the Living Collection. Here you will find a variety of species, some quite exotic, amongst some more local inhabitants that take the opportunity to fly in and enjoy some of the home comforts. Here you will find the nene goose (also known as the Hawaiian goose, top left). Its not an exaggeration to say that Sir Peter Scott, the founder of WWT, saved this rather friendly and inquisitive bird from extinction. Back in the early 50s there were only 30 left in the wild and wishing to do what he could to save them, he brought a pair back to Slimbridge and now, over 60 years later, after a reintroduction programme there are more 2,000 in Hawaii.

**Top Right:** Common pochard. **Bottom Right:** Southern screamers from South America. **Bottom Left:** A pair of whistling ducks and a Egyptian goose.

**Top Left:** Hooded merganser. **Top Right:** Moorhen making the best use of the surroundings. During 2021 some artists have been displaying their work around the reserve and I'm not sure how much they wanted the locals to interact but it seems perfect to me. **Bottom:** A smew - The old English name for a smew is 'White Nun'

# Cranes

The demoiselle crane is from eastern Europe and Asia. A migratory bird, those from Europe winter in Africa and those from Asia, winter in India.

# A day in the life of a BIRDER

My name is Roger Mantell.

I am a retired shipping director and am passionate about bird watching.

**I am a birder.**

Where I am at my happiest is strolling around a nature reserve, open countryside or seashore with my binoculars and high zoom bridge camera in hand, quietly observing and photographing birds and other wildlife.

All birders have a local patch. I am very lucky to have my local patch at the London Wetland Centre, Barnes.

I normally arrive at the reserve mid-morning. The first thing I do is to look on the board outside the visitor centre to see which birds have been sighted on that and previous days. From the visitor centre I then walk along the South route. This takes me past reed beds which in spring-time are alive with the song of reed and sedge warblers, and also with the unmistakable penetrating song of the cetti's warbler, which has now become a year-round resident.

After a short distance to the left are the Dulverton and WWT hides which overlook the main lake of the reserve. From there I can see year-round birds such as tufted, gadwall and mallard ducks, Canada and greylag geese, cormorants, great crested & occasionally little grebes, pied wagtails, different species of gulls, summer common terns and occasionally shelducks and pintails. During a visit a few years ago I was lucky enough to see a black tern hawking over the lake. I have had my best views of the wintering bitterns from these hides.

The next stop is the bird feeder area where there are usually blue and great tits, greenfinches and chaffinches. A brambling has occasionally been seen here in winter, but I've yet to see one.

From here I wander quietly along the path on the far side of the Sheltered lagoon. This is a wonderful place for springtime bird song. It is best to stop and listen in order to have the chance of seeing beautiful songsters such as blackcaps, chiffchaffs, goldfinches and wrens. From the lagoon reed beds there is again the chattering metallic song of the reed warblers and the slightly more musical version of the sedge warblers. In winter redwings and fieldfares can be seen in this area.

I then arrive at the Wader scrape hide overlooking the Wader scrape, where water levels are controlled to encourage visits from passing waders during the migration seasons, and the breeding of waders such as lapwings. The highlight here though is a good view of the sand martin nest bank. It's wonderful to see the aerial acrobatics of these birds, and well as of house martins, although the latter have been scarce this year, also of swifts and the occasional swallow.

The next stop and the highlight of the reserve is the 2-story Peacock hide. It is bordered by the main lake, the Sheltered lagoon, the Wader scrape and the Grazing marsh with the Reservoir lagoon in the distance. The best views are from the second floor. In the distance to the north is Charing Cross Hospital, on the roof of which are breeding peregrine falcons, which feed on wild life on the reserve. On occasions I have seen one sitting on a rail on the outside of the hospital.

Some birders and photographers, loaded down with heavy equipment, head straight for this hide, set up their telescopes, cameras and tripods and spend most of the time of their visit there. If a rare bird is passing through there is quite a number of people. The snipes on the Grazing marsh are always a highlight. There is a long list of migrant and rare birds sighted from this hide,

and included amongst those I have seen are common and green sandpipers, Iceland gulls, little ringed plovers, oyster catchers, redshanks, wheatears, whimbrels, yellow wagtails and singles of an avocet, merlin, ring ouzel and short-eared owl. There are many grey herons which are seen from here, and in winter there are large numbers of shoveler, teal and wigeon ducks. There is also a guide in the hide to point out interesting birds. Everyone is very friendly, which is common with birders. Those with telescopes invite you to look through their lenses.

I then make my way back to the visitor centre taking the path on the near side of the Sheltered lagoon, from where I have seen kingfishers, although not in recent years. I arrive in time for an excellent lunch in the restaurant, following which I take the path towards the West route.  Here I go through the World Wetlands, the captive bird area. Many birders do not bother with these captive birds, but I am always interested in looking at some of the very colourful species.

At the corner of this area is the Headley hide. It overlooks the main lake on the western side.  Again there is sometimes a guide in the hide. There is also a feeder station which you can see through the glass, where reed buntings often feed.

Then I pass through a double gate into Wildside. This is a wooded, beautifully tranquil area, interspersed by small lakes, where I slowly walk, watching and listening to the wonderful sounds of nature. It is difficult to believe that London is so near. It feels like being in the middle of the countryside. There is another reed bed area here. Finally I arrive at the Wildside hide which looks out over the Reservoir lagoon. As well as the other wildfowl already mentioned there are common pochards.  It is in this area where I have seen the reserve's sparrowhawks.

I then return to the restaurant for coffee and cake – a perfect day!

**Roger Mantell**

**Inset:** Some of Roger's sightings. **Opposite Left:** Greenshank.
**This Page, Top to Bottom:**  Short-eared owl, pintail and snipes.

# Around the Reserve

**This Page, Below Left:** A new introduction in 2020 were the sheep which were gifted to the reserve by a local supporter. They help to keep the grasses in top condition and save a lot of mowing.

**Below Right:** Green woodpeckers are regular visitors to the reserve but are very shy, so you will rarely see them for long.

**Opposite Page Top:** The sheltered lagoon.

**Opposite Page Bottom:** Canada geese.

# Coming to the Reserve

In normal times, there are always special events on. Always a hit with the children is when the people from The Falconry School come with their collection of birds of prey.

The reserve is a photographer's dream with not only wildlife to see but also perfect landscapes with big skies, like the day I was joined by my photographic friends, Sarah Longes and Sophie Carr (this page, top). If you are lucky, the wildlife will come to you and even sit on your equipment, as this Robin did the day I was joined by my good friend, Tammy Marlar (this page bottom). The otters are always a draw and one can never pass their pen without at least one picture, as on the day I was joined by another good friend, Simon Arron (top right opposite).

# Sparrowhawks

The reserve, sadly acts as a larder for the kings of the food chain and this pair decided to set up home over one of the pools in the Living Collection, where they could literally look down at their breakfast, lunch and dinner. The nest was successful, with at least 3 chicks fledging, one visible in the picture below.

# The Reeds

The large areas of reeds you see at the reserve are not just there for decoration, they serve a multitude of purposes. As well as providing a wonderful habitat for fish, invertebrates and birds such as warblers (see the next few pages) they also help to clean the water by removing harmful elements and oxygenating it at the same time. They need a lot of attention to keep them healthy and areas are regularly cut-back to let new growth through, pictures bottom left and right. If that wasn't enough, they also have a part to play in helping with flood prevention, which is becoming ever more important as the effects of climate change begin to bite, especially in our cities. Besides the warblers, you can also spot reed buntings at the reserve, below centre.

It is always a wonderful moment at the reserve when the reed warblers return from their wintering grounds in sub Saharan Africa; their beautiful song echoing out from amongst the reeds as you walk the paths of the reserve. That said, they are a devil to photograph and you need lots of patience, as they are hard to see and the reeds have a tendency to get in the way.

# Summer

The joyous arrival of the swifts and sand martins in the air is a sure sign that summer has arrived. Amongst the many species seen across the reserve in summer, the smaller Damselflies could be missed but are numerous at this time of year. They are graceful fliers with their slender bodies and long filmy net-veined wings and are found mainly near shallow freshwater habitats. Their bodies are of iridescent blue or red and the females usually have a golden-brown colour on their wing.

As the summer progresses, the grass is cut across the site, with the hay used to feed the cows and sheep during the winter months. Once the wildflower meadows have finished flowering and gone to seed, the vegetation is cut back, which discourages unwanted invasive species and helps to maintain the level nutrients in the soil.

WWT in Barnes is a fabulous venue for a wedding , as I discovered in early August 2021 when I chanced upon Ellie and Rob celebrating in the courtyard. Left picture courtesy of Jennifer West Photography (www.jenniferwestweddings.com)

Summer will always be my favourite season, but even more so at London Wetland Centre. The otters bask in the sun, dragonflies dance, and everything glistens in the sunshine. Everyone is in a good mood, and I love seeing people relax with drinks sitting by our pond, and children playing in our rain showers. Summer is just magical.

**LISA WOODWARD**
Centre Manager

# Black-headed gulls

These feisty birds have been a huge success on the reserve and are quite happy to rob other birds of their meal if they can, here chasing a great crested grebe.

The black-headed gulls take up most of the space on the rafts and islands, where they breed very successfully, to the exclusion of the poor terns.

In 2021 some of the rafts were raided by herons but the gulls that nested on the islands faired better, as there was more cover for the young.

147

Many birds have two broods each year but if spring arrives late then they will only produce one family.
**This Page:** Mallards. **Below Right & Opposite Bottom:** Tufted ducks. **Opposite Top:** Grey-lag geese.

**Opposite Page:**
**Top Left and Bottom:** Grey-lag geese.
**Right Top:** A coot.
**Right Middle and Bottom:** This was something unusual but not unheard of, where a moorhen juvenile from the first brood helps out the parents with the second.

**This page:**
**Top:** Moorhen.
**Bottom:** Little grebes. As with their larger cousins, the little grebe babies ride on their parents backs for the first few days. The parents feed them roughage, for instance feathers, to help them digest the fish, particularly the bones. They then regurgitate the left-overs in the form of pellets.

# Birds from around the Reserve

The very nature of the reserve attracts many wetland birds but also many land lubbers too, so it was fun to catch this family of long-tailed tits amongst the bushes (opposite, bottom right).

**Opposite Top Left:** I caught some lapwings mating. This is not a sight you catch that often as it is very quick – one blink and it's over.

**Opposite Top Right:** A family of Canada geese from the Wild Side strayed onto a swan's patch, where they were nesting, and their goslings dived out of the way as the parents caught the brunt the male swan's anger. Thankfully all escaped unharmed.

**This Page:** The reserve had a pair of oyster catchers nest for the first time this year (2021) but sadly the nest didn't succeed. Within half a day the chicks ended up as a meal for some of the larger resident gulls, sadly before I could get a glimpse.

**Opposite:** Coot Island. I know these do very well on the reserve but I think this picture proves it.

**Below Bottom:** Feeding time can always be a good moment to catch some action when visiting the Living Collection.

# Egrets & Herons

The egret is an occasional visitor to the reserve and a pair were around in the summer of 2021 and what beautiful birds they are. Little egrets are part of the heron family and as our climate has warmed they have become regular visitors in the summer, with some even wintering here in the south.

As with the egrets, the grey herons form colonies of nests in trees. However, with there being few suitable trees at the reserve, the nearest heronry is at the Leg o'Mutton Nature Reserve down Lonsdale Road in Barnes. But the herons visit the Centre as there is plenty for them to eat, from fish and frogs to young birds.

# Mute Swans

There are several pairs of swans on the reserve, many of which have successful broods each year. Swans are very territorial and do not tolerate other birds around them, especially Canada geese, when they are nesting or have young. Although their name derives from them being less vocal than other swans, they still make their presence known and like the great crested grebes, they have a dramatic courtship dance.

**Below Right:** Image by Tammy Marlar. I was there that day but recorded a video, so had no still image of my own.

# Kingfishers

There are several kingfishers that consider the reserve home, but you have to count yourself extremely lucky to see them. They are very shy, choose to nest far from the gaze of any hide but are the most colourful and gorgeous bird.

Gulls and other birds of prey are not the only menace that the ground nesting birds have to contend with, there are also the resident foxes. They don't seem to mind the water and can cause a major panic when they stride through the reserve. You have to feel sorry for the pair of lapwings, below, who may well have lost their eggs or young in this raid.

# Everything's Coming Up Daisies

The swing from spring to summer is greeted across the reserve with a wonderful display of ox-eye daisies, attracting a whole array of visitors.

**Clockwise from Top Left:** Ladybird, banded demoiselle damselfly, mallard duck, rose chafer beetle, crab spider, painted lady butterfly and thick-legged beetle.

167

# Summer Flowers

Something to rival the wonderful water fowl, are the flowers that pop up all over the reserve in summer. **Below Left:** Bee orchid. **Below Middle:** Pyramid orchid. **Bottom:** Southern marsh orchid amongst birds-foot trefoils (and also opposite with an Essex skipper butterfly). **Overleaf:** The beautiful fleabane with a gatekeeper butterfly.

# Butterflies

With the flowers come the butterflies: a common blue (opposite) red admiral (right) and Essex skipper (below).

**Left:** My personal favourite, the marbled white.
**Top:** Speckled wood. **Middle:** Common blue. **Bottom:** Ringlet.

**Opposite:** Small white.

**Below:** Six spot burnet day-flying moth.

**Right:** The beautiful brimstone.

# Dragonflies

**This Page and Overleaf:** The southern hawker is a large species of dragonfly and usually found near water. It is a strong flyer and will venture further afield in search of insect prey. Their aquatic larvae take up to three years to develop.

There are about 30 species of dragonfly in the UK and the reserve offers most of them the perfect habitat with plenty of water for breeding and for attracting their prey.

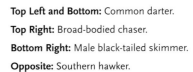

**Top Left and Bottom:** Common darter.

**Top Right:** Broad-bodied chaser.

**Bottom Right:** Male black-tailed skimmer.

**Opposite:** Southern hawker.

# Bringing in the Hay

Although cattle and sheep have been introduced to try and keep the grass growth in check, each September, the team on the reserve work hard to cut the grass and help provide some valuable hay for use with the animals. Clearly the cows haven't seen that many tractors and had a good sniff when they came by.

# Volunteering

The team of dedicated volunteers are vital to the work of WWT. They're involved in all areas of the charity, including assisting customers, caring for wildfowl, recruiting new members, helping with conservation record keeping and much, much more. So if the pictures in this book have inspired you to know more and to possibly help with their work do please get in touch either through the website **wwt.org.uk/volunteer** or enquire in any of the shops.

# Lizards & Snakes

Common lizards can be found all over the reserve, loving nothing better than to bask in the sun, particularly on the wooden bridge supports in the Wild Side and on the piles of tiles dotted around the South Side.

The other reptiles found on the site are slow worms and grass snakes which are rarely seen as they are pretty shy. I was fortunate some years ago to join a party around the reserve led by the well-known TV presenter and photographer Mark Carwardine and one of the bonuses was to be taken behind the scenes to see some of these wonderful creatures up close.

# Around the Reserve

**Top Right:** The bee wolf, which preys upon honey bees and buries them in the ground as food for their larvae; fascinating if not a little macabre.
**Middle Left:** Carnivorous pitcher plants, which can be found in the kids zone.

**Bottom Left:** A cormorant drying out its feathers. **Bottom Right:** The pair of Bewick's swans are always a popular feature in the Living Collection but due to Covid they were removed. Hopefully they will return soon.

# The Last Day of Summer

The otters at play, and asleep in their holt, marsh frogs basking in the late summer sun, moorhens playing with the new art installation, a pair of damselflies and some socially distanced gulls.

# Autumn

In autumn, the vegetation growth on the main islands of the lake is cut back. This is to open the areas and encourage waders and wintering waterfowl to arrive during their annual autumn visit. This also helps to manage the condition of the soil, as wildflowers prefer a less nutrient rich soil.

Despite a huge array of pictures in this book, in reality its only a fraction of the wildlife that comes here, many just passing through. So I was grateful to a lady on Twitter, @Kazbel, who kindly shared this picture of a Godwit she caught in the Living Collection.

I used to love spring but since getting a decent camera I'd say autumn is my favourite season because of the rich colours.

**FRANK GARDNER**
Broadcaster and President of the
British Trust for Ornithology

# Around the Reserve

When the full force of autumn colour hits the reserve, the landscape is transformed into a patchwork of vibrant reds, oranges and golds.

Visiting the animals in the Living Collection is always a highlight for school trips, but be warned, the geese eat anything, even your trousers!

# Wetlands can be good for your mental health and general wellbeing.

Some new YouGov research, released by the Mental Health Foundation in 2021, found that 65 % of people found that being near water improved their mental wellbeing and was their favourite part of nature. Those of us who love WWT already knew this of course, but it is good to have science back it up.

# Fungi

One of the highlights of autumn is the arrival of fungi, which pop up all over the reserve, even on some of the benches.

All rights reserved. No part of this publication may be reproduced, stored in any retrieval system or transmitted in any form or by any means, electronic, mechanical photocopying or otherwise without the prior permission of the copyright holders. Whilst every care has been taken in the production of this book, no responsibility can be accepted for any errors or omissions. The publishers have taken all reasonable care in compiling this work but cannot accept responsibility for the information derived from third parties, which has been reproduced in good faith.

First Edition – © Unity Print and Publishing Limited 2021

Historian: Caroline MacMillan
*www.westlondonwalks.co.uk*

Designed by Ascent Creative
*www.ascent-creative.co.uk*

Printed by Page Bros in Norwich
*www.pagebros.co.uk*

Bound by Green St Bindery of Oxford
*www.maltbysbookbinders.co.uk*

Colour Management by Paul Sherfield of The Missing Horse Consultancy.
*www.missinghorsecons.co.uk*

Publishing assistant: Josie Wilson

Published by Unity Print and Publishing Limited,
18 Dungarvan Avenue,
London SW15 5QU.

Tel: +44 (0)20 8487 2199
*aw@unity-publishing.co.uk*
*www.wildlondon.co.uk*

Endpapers taken from The National Library of Scotland, dated 1919.

My son complains that he never appears in my books, to which I answer, well you never come out with me (his sister is in many of them and loves her photography) . Well, I came across this old picture from a visit we made in 2009 and thought I would share it.

Andrew uses a Canon 6D camera and accessories plus an iPhone 11

Follow Andrew on the socials:
Twitter and Instagram @wildlondonpics